My FIRST AID Guide to...

FAINTING AND SEIZURES

by Joanna Brundle

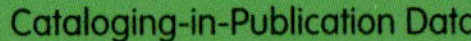

Published in 2022 by
KidHaven Publishing, an Imprint of Greenhaven Publishing, LLC
353 3rd Avenue
Suite 255
New York, NY 10010

Edited by: William Anthony
Designed by: Laura Gatie

Find us on

Cataloging-in-Publication Data

Names: Brundle, Joanna.
Title: Fainting and seizures / Joanna Brundle.
Description: New York : KidHaven Publishing, 2022. | Series: My first aid guide to… | Includes glossary and index.
Identifiers: ISBN 9781534538146 (pbk.) | ISBN 9781534538160 (library bound) | ISBN 9781534538153 (6 pack) | ISBN 9781534538177 (ebook)
Subjects: LCSH: Spasms--Juvenile literature. | Epilepsy--Juvenile literature. | Syncope (Pathology)--Juvenile literature. | First aid in illness and injury--Juvenile literature.
Classification: LCC RC429.B78 2022 | DDC 616.02'5--dc23

Printed in the United States of America

CPSIA compliance information: Batch #CSKH22: For further information contact Greenhaven Publishing LLC, New York, New York at 1-844-317-7404.

Please visit our website, www.greenhavenpublishing.com. For a free color catalog of all our high-quality books, call toll free 1-844-317-7404 or fax 1-844-317-7405.

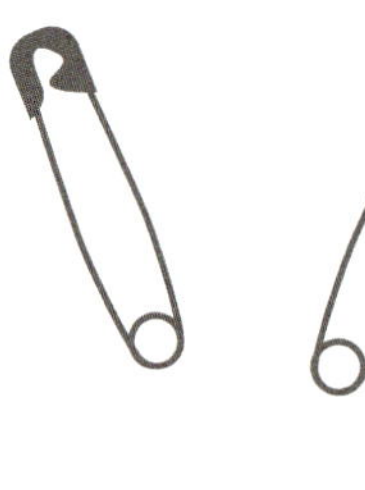

Photo Credits

All images are courtesy of Shutterstock.com, unless otherwise specified. With thanks to Getty Images, Thinkstock Photo, and iStockphoto.

Cover - Borysevych.com, Asya.L, AlenKadr, LeventeGyori, Aha-Soft, New Africa, Kwangmoozaa, piotr_pabijan, LightField Studios, Africa Studio, Flas100. Whiteboard - piotr_pabijan. Grid - world of vector. Page number plasters - Nik Merkulov. Bandage headings - Africa Studio. 1 - elenabsl, LightField Studios. 2 - iLoveCoffeeDesign, elenabsl. 3 - elenabsl, M.Stasy, iLoveCoffeeDesign. 4 - M.Stasy, Flas100, heartor, Aha-Soft. 5 - Vectomart, Photographee.eu, Aha-Soft. 6 - Akkalak Aiempradit, Flas100, Aha-Soft. 7 - CGN089, Aha-Soft, Flas100. 8 - sunabesyou, elenabsl. 9 - M.Stasy, Flas100, Africa Studio, Aha-Soft, BATKA. 10 - Vectomart, Photographee.eu. 11 - Monkey Business Images, Aha-Soft, elenabsl, Flas100. 12 - Goldsithney, Katrina Lee. 13 - Tunatura, Aha-Soft, Flas100. 14 - Goldsithney, Flas100, elenabsl, Aha-Soft. 15 - marco mayer, Aha-Soft. 16 - ZoranOrcik. 17 - Littlekidmoment, Aha-Soft. 18 - Anton Papulov, Vectomart, Aha-Soft. 19 - SpeedKingz, Aha-Soft, Vectomart. 20 - kdshutterman, elenabsl, Flas100. 21 - OgnjenO, elenabsl, Flas100. 22 - Vitalii Petrushenko elenabsl, iLoveCoffeeDesign. 23 - Monkey Business Images, Aha-Soft. 24 - elenabsl, iLoveCoffeeDesign.

CONTENTS

Words that look like this can be found in the glossary on page 24.

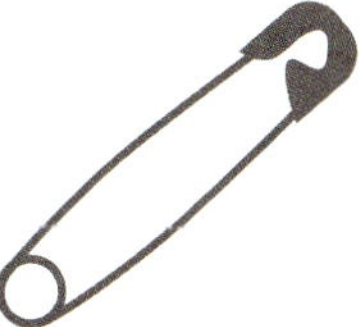

WHAT IS FIRST AID?

First aid is the help that is given to someone right after they have hurt themselves, had an accident, or become sick. Anyone can give first aid, including you.

This girl is being helped by her friend.

Learning simple first aid is important. You will learn how to help someone who is sick or injured and what to do in a medical emergency. You may even save someone's life.

WHAT IS FAINTING?

When someone loses consciousness for a short time, we call it fainting. A person who is about to faint usually feels weak and wobbly before losing consciousness and falling down.

Fainting is caused by less blood than normal flowing to the brain.

Warning signs that someone is about to faint include yawning, sudden sweating, and fast, deep breathing. The person may feel sick and have ringing in their ears.

WHAT HAPPENS WHEN SOMEONE FAINTS?

Fainting can be brought on by sudden pain or by being very thirsty, hungry, tired, or upset. People sometimes faint if it is very hot, especially if they have been standing or sitting still for a long time.

When someone faints, they may have a low heart rate (pulse). Their skin may be pale, cold, and sweaty. They should regain consciousness quickly, but they might feel confused and weak for a while.

You can check someone's pulse by feeling their wrist for regular beats.

HELPING SOMEONE WHO FEELS FAINT

If someone feels faint, help them to lie down and then kneel down beside them. Help them to lift up their legs. Support their ankles on a chair or on your shoulder.

Lifting a person's legs helps the blood flow back to the brain.

Make sure the person has plenty of fresh air. If you are inside, open some windows. The person should start to <u>recover</u> quickly. Talk to them calmly and help them sit up slowly.

If a person who faints hasn't woken up after two minutes, call an ambulance.

WHAT ARE SEIZURES?

Lots of things are happening inside our brains all the time. Seizures happen when there is unusual activity in the brain. They only affect some people, but can happen whether the person is awake or asleep.

Someone having a seizure may become unconscious. Their body may go stiff. If they are standing, they may fall down. Their back may be arched and they may have difficult, unusual breathing.

The person may make jerky, uncontrolled movements. They may have clenched teeth and saliva (spit) coming from their mouth. If they have bitten their tongue or cheek during the seizure, the saliva may have blood in it.

There may be warning signs that someone is about to have a seizure. The person may feel confused, sick, dizzy, or worried. Some people have a headache or feel tingling or <u>numbness</u> in parts of their body.

WHAT CAUSES SEIZURES?

Epilepsy is a condition that affects some people's brains. It is the most common cause of seizures. Triggers are the things that bring on an epileptic seizure. They can include flashing lights, video games, and lack of sleep.

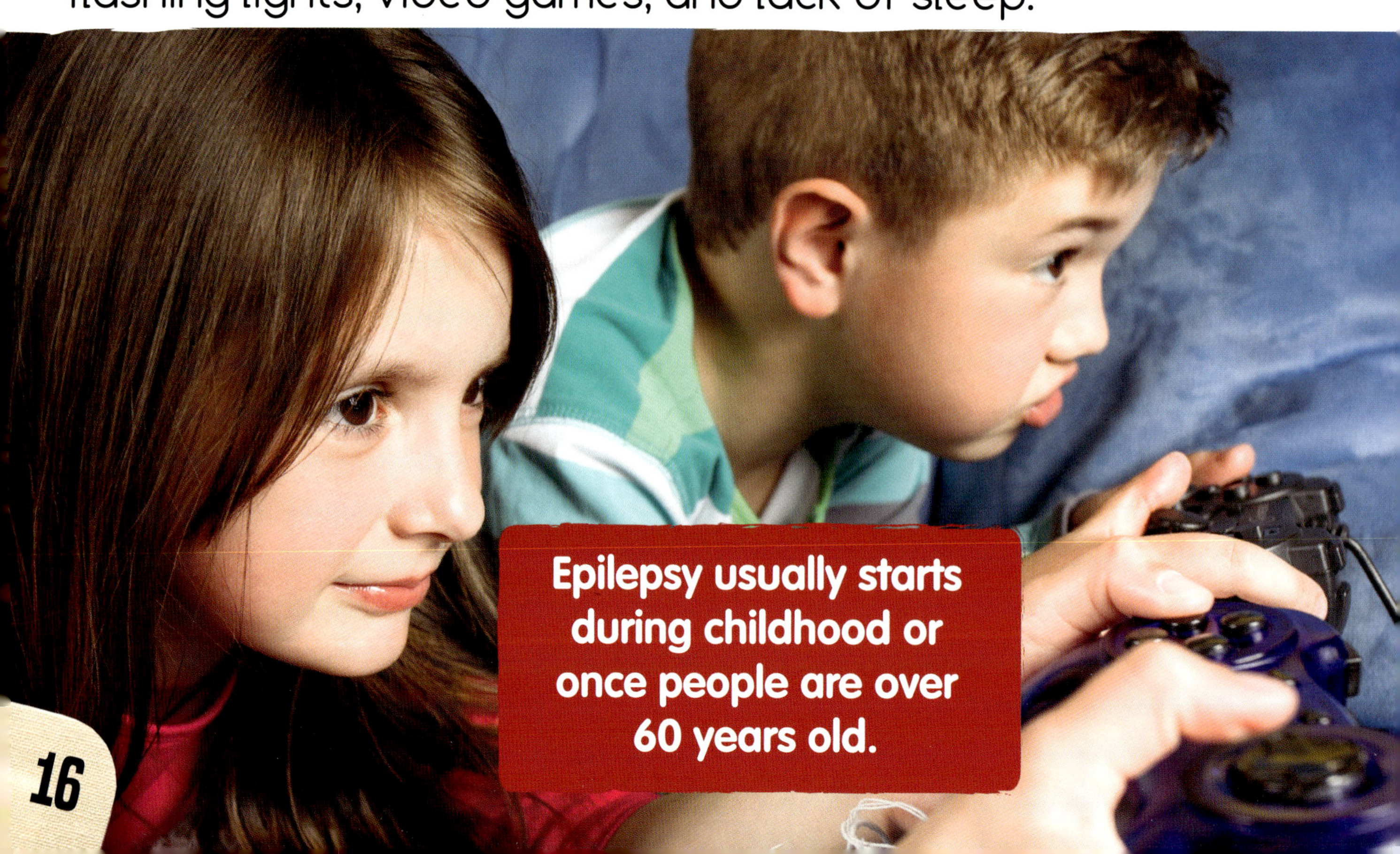

Epilepsy usually starts during childhood or once people are over 60 years old.

Seizures can affect someone with a head injury or very high temperature.

Diabetes is a condition that affects the amount of sugar in the blood. Diabetic people may have a seizure if their blood sugar level falls too low.

HELPING SOMEONE WHO IS HAVING A SEIZURE

If someone is having a seizure, move away anything that could hurt them, such as hot drinks or sharp objects. Protect the person's head using a cushion or your coat. Loosen any clothes around their neck.

Make a note of the time when a seizure starts so you know how long it lasts.

Don't try to move the person or stop their jerky movements. Don't put anything in their mouth. When the seizure is over, talk to them calmly. Stay with them until they feel completely better.

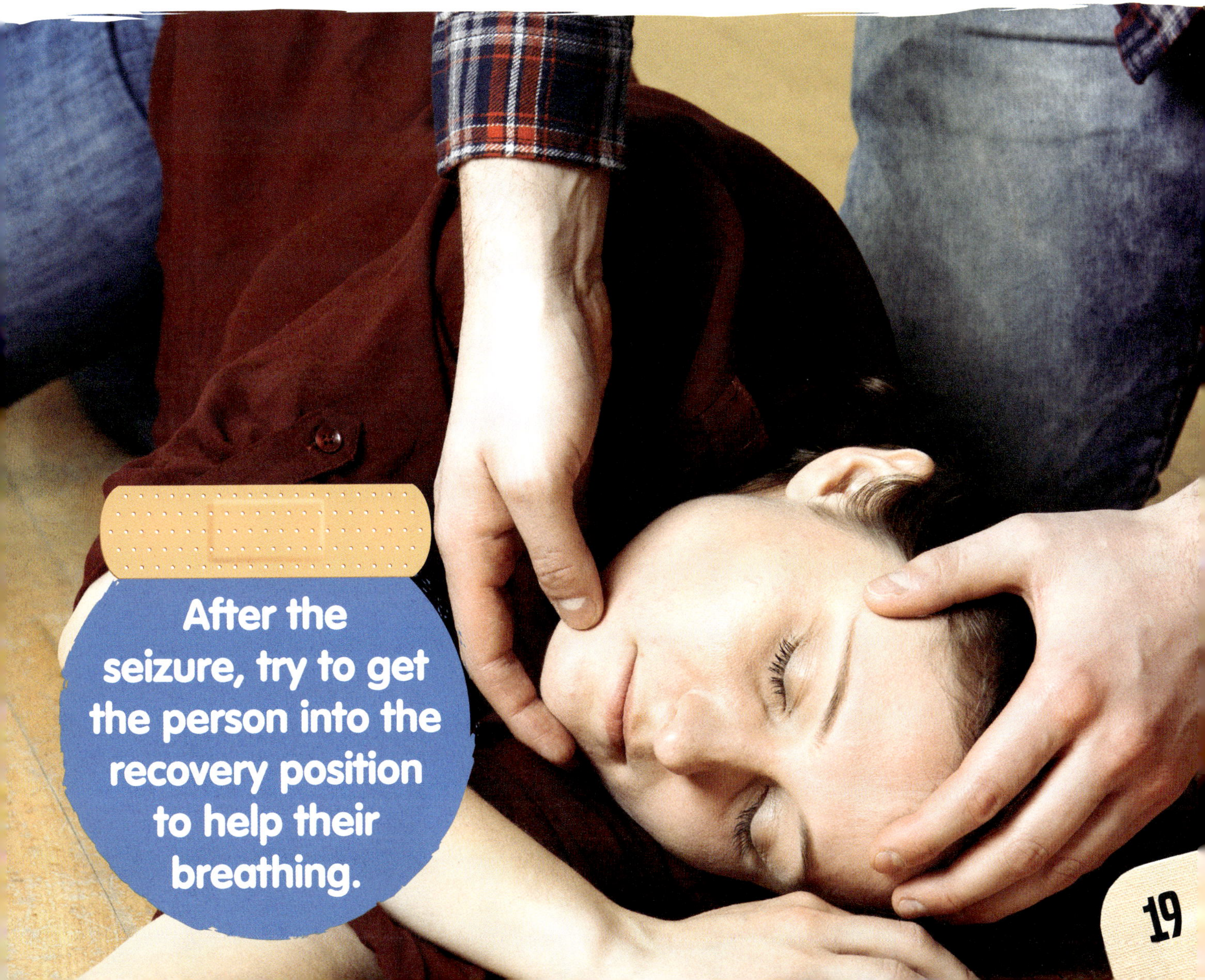

After the seizure, try to get the person into the recovery position to help their breathing.

CALL AN AMBULANCE!

Always call an ambulance if:

The reason for the seizure is not known

The person has had an injury or has injured themselves during the seizure

The person is having several seizures, one after another

The seizure lasts for more than five minutes

The person is having their first seizure

The person is not responsive for more than ten minutes

You are worried about the person's breathing

THINGS TO REMEMBER

You can call an ambulance by dialling 911 from any home phone or cell phone. Tell the operator where you are and that you need an ambulance.

Try to stay as calm as you can. It will help you to follow the operator's instructions.

Someone who has fainted or had a seizure should not be left alone. Stay with them until an ambulance comes or the person feels better.

GLOSSARY

condition an illness, disease, or injury

consciousness an alert state in which someone is awake and aware of what is happening

heart rate (pulse) the number of times someone's heart beats in one minute

medical emergency a situation in which someone needs help from a medical professional right away

numbness not being able to feel anything

operator the person who answers an emergency telephone call

recover to feel better

regular happening in an even, fixed pattern

responsive able to answer a question or follow an instruction, such as "open your eyes"

unconscious not being awake or aware of what is happening

INDEX